AF552836

SRI SRI PARAMAHANSA YOGANANDA
(1893-1952)
Gurudeva and Founder
Yogoda Satsanga Society of India/
Self-Realization Fellowship

Habit—Your Master or Your Slave?

and Other Lectures

By

Sri Sri Paramahansa Yogananda

"He is the wisest who seeks God. He is the most successful who has found God."

— *Sri Sri Paramahansa Yogananda*

First Indian Edition, 1979
Sixth Impression, 2021

An authorized publication of Yogoda Satsanga Society of India/Self-Realization Fellowship

The Yogoda Satsanga Society of India name and emblem shown above appear on all YSS books, recordings, and other publications, assuring the reader that a work originates with the society established by Sri Sri Paramahansa Yogananda and faithfully conveys his teachings.

Published in India by
YOGODA SATSANGA SOCIETY OF INDIA
Yogoda Satsanga Math
21, U. N. Mukherjee Road
Dakshineswar, Kolkata 700076

Printed in India by
Kailash Paper Conversion Pvt. Ltd.
Ranchi 834001

ISBN 978-81-89535-30-8

Distributed by:

 Jaico Publishing House  Manjul Publishing House

Also available from Yogoda Satsanga Society of India, Paramahansa Yogananda Path, Ranchi 834001, Jharkhand and at Yogoda Satsanga Ashrams and Dhyana Kendras throughout India.

PREFACE

From the embryonic period of man's reason he has sought to understand the mysteries of his existence and the nature of his Creator. Enlightenment on these matters has been the special mission of wise men in every age. Realizing this, the ideal of *satsanga* (company with the good and the wise) has rooted itself in the very core of India's spiritual tradition. From *satsanga* the *sadhak* gathers inspiration and advances his spiritual understanding. The more divine the good company is, the more the *sadhak* can absorb from the experience. But only a fortunate few have the rare and blessed opportunity to be actually in the personal company of a truly great soul. The seeking masses are denied this privilege if we take literally the concept of *satsanga* as the necessity to be in the physical presence of the saint. If, however, we realise that the intrinsic value of *satsanga* is in the ability of the devotee to be receptive to the teachings and guidance of the saint, whether or not the *sadhak* be in the physical company of that divine soul, the modern medium of the printed word brings the upliftment of *satsanga* to the *sadhana* of every seeker.

It is in this spirit that *Habit—Your Master or Your Slave?* is offered to the reader.

His Holiness Sri Sri Paramahansa Yogananda, who speaks to you in the pages of this booklet, entered mahasamadhi on March 7, 1952. The remarkable incorruptibility of his body after death was a continued reflection of his unique, spiritually transcendent life. He is the revered Guru-founder of the now worldwide institution of Yogoda Satsanga Society of India/Self-Realization Fellowship. The basis of his teaching is *Raja Yoga*, the ancient, universal science of soul-realization. The Society carries on its activities and spreads the teachings of Sri Sri Paramahansa Yogananda through publication of his books and writings, including confidential spiritual lessons; and through the medium of branch centres, and educational and charitable institutions. If this booklet is the reader's first introduction to Sri Sri Paramahansa Yogananda and the Society he founded, the experience of *satsanga* with the blessed Guru in these pages may well be the beginning of a deeper acquaintance and continuing relationship.

The worth of any writing consists in its ability to convey the intended message; the authority of the message lies in the qualifications of the writer. The contents of this booklet will speak for itself; the authority of the author is readily confirmed by a thoughtful perusal of *Autobiography of a Yogi,* the life testimony of one to whom Truth was not fact but realization.

The Publishers
YOGODA SATSANGA SOCIETY OF INDIA

The Spiritual Legacy of Sri Sri Paramahansa Yogananda

His Complete Writings, Lectures, and Informal Talks

Paramahansa Yogananda founded Yogoda Satsanga Society of India (YSS) in 1917 and Self-Realization Fellowship (SRF) in 1920 to disseminate his teachings worldwide and to preserve their purity and integrity for generations to come. A prolific writer and lecturer from his earliest years in America, he created a renowned and voluminous body of works on the yoga science of meditation, the art of balanced living, and the underlying unity of all great religions. Today this unique and far-reaching spiritual legacy lives on, inspiring millions of truth seekers all over the world.

In accord with the express wishes of the great Guru, Yogoda Satsanga Society of India/Self-Realization Fellowship has continued the ongoing task of publishing and keeping permanently in print *The Complete Works of Paramahansa Yogananda.* These include not only the final editions of all the books he published during his lifetime, but also many new titles—works that had remained unpublished at the time of his passing in 1952, or which had been serialized over the years in incomplete form in Yogoda Satsanga Society of India/Self-Realization Fellowship's magazine, as well as hundreds of profoundly inspiring lectures and informal talks recorded but not printed before his passing.

Paramahansa Yogananda personally chose and trained those close disciples who formed the Yogoda Satsanga Society of India/Self-Realization Fellowship Publications Council, giving them specific guidelines for the preparation and publishing of his teachings. The members of the YSS/SRF Publications Council (monks and nuns who have taken lifelong vows of renunciation and selfless service) honour these guidelines as a sacred trust, in order that the universal message of this beloved world teacher will live on in its original power and authenticity.

The Yogoda Satsanga Society of India/Self-Realization Fellowship emblem (shown on previous page) was designated by Paramahansa Yogananda to identify the nonprofit society he founded as the authorized source of his teachings. The YSS/SRF name and emblem appear on all YSS/SRF publications and recordings, assuring the reader that a work originates with the organization founded by Paramahansa Yogananda and conveys his teachings as he himself intended they be given.

—Yogoda Satsanga Society of India/
Self-Realization Fellowship

CONTENTS

Habit—Your Master or Your Slave?

Date and place unknown

The human brain, with its hilly ranges of cerebral convolutions inlaid with arterial streamlets and dark rivers of veins, presents an epitome of a huge estate. Is this exquisite territory devoid of a Divine Resident? Could there be a book without an author, a child without parents, a clock without a maker, a rose without a designer? Nay! Similarly, the cerebral domain of mystic beauty has been shaped by wondrous intelligent agencies.

Who lives in this marvellous hall whose walls of mortared osseous tissues are fitted with ocular, tactual, auditory, olfactory, and gustatory doors? Beneath the dome of the human skull a colony of myriads of cells pulsating with life and intelligence are playing out scenes of intense activity. Tiny brain cells are engaged in diverse pursuits—banqueting, introspecting, and receiving guests of sensations that enter from the outer sensory doors. There is buying and selling going on: processes of absorption and elimination. Like tiny boats, blood corpuscles paddle along arterial streams, laden with various vital commodities.

Guiding and controlling many of these cellular activities is an unseen band of impish pixies and good fairies—habits. Sometimes great mischief is created when foreign and lawless habits are permitted entry into the cranial commonwealth. They set themselves up as lords, dominating the activities of their hosts, the brain cells. When the latter attempt to resist this encroachment on their freedom, these United States of Flesh become a scene of civil war. The whole bodily country is thrown into disorder while the brain cells furiously debate the right of certain habits to act as petty dictators.

How do habits gain power to tyrannise over human conduct? Every human activity, whether it be performed as an outward physical movement or as an inner process of thought, is a vote for a particular habit. Repetition of that action or thought swells the number of votes in favour of electing that habit to a seat in the bodily government. A considerable number of such actions vote that habit into office. At different periods of life a collective vote of all previous human actions determines which habits are going to predominate and rule supreme.

An election by numerical superiority alone, without adherence to a desirable qualitative standard, may bring disaster upon a country. If the majority of voters are morons or criminals, they are bound to blunder and elect the wrong president. Similarly, unless the votes of human actions are cast according to the supreme law of discrimination, the brain cells may thoughtlessly enslave themselves under tyrannical habit-dictators.

Maintenance of a truly enlightened spiritual democracy in the bodily country requires a thorough education of the brain-cell citizenry. The latter should be trained not to permit habit-candidates to be elected merely on the numerical strength of thoughtlessly repeated actions, but should consciously exercise the qualitative power of discriminative attention with the casting of every action-vote. They should be guided by ideal rationalism, and heed its warnings against accepting the bribe of sentimental attachment to environment, which leads to the misuse of voting power. Discriminative reason should be the sole guide in selection of the presidential habit-candidates.

Are Habit Slaves Born or Made?

Habits of drinking, excessive smoking, overindulgence in coffee or tea; and habitual moods of anger, greed, envy, sloth, and despondency are usually elected to office by the cumulative numerical strength of unwise hordes of little actions performed without any thought of the after-effect of enslavement. Persons addicted to such habits are not born ineluctably to their unfortunate fate; in this or in a past life, knowingly or unknowingly, they have enslaved themselves through constant repetition of certain actions. The first drink never made a drunkard; the first act of sensuality never made a libertine; the first use of narcotics never made a dope addict. It was a series of mechanical or ill-considered repetitions of such misguided actions that elected these gripping habits to power.* Quantitative strength won against the qualitative voice of attentive reason, which had become weakened through failure to exercise its powers, and had thus lost its vote.

Guard yourself, therefore, against the first performance of a wrong act. What you do once you are likely to do again. It is by repetition that a habit grows stronger and bigger, like a rolling snowball. Use your reason in all your actions; otherwise you may thoughtlessly convert yourself into a helpless slave of undesirable habits.

* For people who have established in previous lives the pattern of a harmful habit, such as alcoholism, the "first drink" was taken many lives ago; that is why in this life even the first drink can revive that habit with alarming suddenness and often tragic consequences.

Impeach a Bad Habit-President and Install a Good One

A strong bad habit presiding for a long time over the bodily country brings chaos and misery. Spiritual famine, mental fevers, and a universal poverty of body and mind exist in that misruled land. A strong bad habit should be impeached before a tribunal of daily introspection under the presiding judge of conscience, who should inform the court of reason that the inevitable outcome of persistence in the offending actions will be an impaired nervous system, wasted powers, and vanished happiness. This constantly sounded note of warning may serve gradually to persuade the jury of reason to the decision to put away forever the guilty victimizing habit.

Sometimes it is difficult to convince the court. Many persons who excessively smoke, drink, or indulge in sex experiences do not seek or even wish to be free of these slavish compulsions. They delusively think that there is nothing harmful about what they are doing because they don't immediately suffer disillusioning painful consequences. Childlike, they fail to visualize the ultimate results of their actions. They do not see that they have set into motion laws that work impartially for good or ill, according to the nature of human actions; that, although the shovels of harmful habits dig slowly, they yet dig surely a yawning, untimely grave, a pit of misery toward which the slave of wrong habits proceeds through scorching flames of suffering. Of such entrapped persons the Gita says: "Harbouring bewildering thoughts, caught in the net of delusion, craving only sensual delights, they sink into a foul hell."*

* Bhagavad Gita XVI:16.

First convince your mind that you are going to overthrow the tyranny of the undesirable ruling habit; then begin the work of constitutional agitation and actual impeachment. A whining or sorrowing attitude, gentle remonstrance, or even violent but spasmodic rebellion is of little avail. It is through continuous repetition of certain actions that you are the maker of your habits; and you must undo hurtful ones by a similarly regular effort, implemented by conscious exercise of will and the discriminative power of reason.

Relate your actions to new and better habits. Keep them continuously busy, interested, and attentive in serving good habits and in fraternizing with other good actions. If your actions begin to revert to their old dangerous habit-influenced associations, don't become discouraged. Persist in right actions, give them sufficient time and attention, and the voting strength of the new good actions will increase and finally become powerful enough to overthrow the worthless habit and to elect in its place a worthy one.

It Takes Time to Establish Habits, Good or Bad

It takes time for even a bad habit to attain supremacy, so why be impatient about the growth of a rival good habit? Do not despair about your undesirable habits; simply stop feeding them and thus making them strong by repetition. The time that elapses in the formation of habits varies with individual nervous systems and brains and is chiefly determined by the quality of one's attention. Through the power of deep, concentration-trained attention, any habit may be installed—that is, new patterns may be made in the brain—almost instantaneously and at will. The potency of concentration and will to create good and bad fortune is strikingly summed up in the Biblical verse: "For whosoever hath, to him shall be given, and he shall have more abundance; but whosoever hath not, from him shall be taken away even that he hath."* This truth is particularly applicable to habits. A man of good actions strengthens his will to perform further good actions, and thus increases in virtue with little effort. But a slave of bad habits debauches his will and reason, so that eventually he is not only powerless to create new good habits, but also has weakened his hold on whatever good habits he may have had at the start.

Government of one's actions by intuitional, wisdom-guided discrimination, uninfluenced by either good or bad habits, imparts unbounded power of will. "But that man succeeds supremely, O Arjuna, who, disciplining the senses by the mind, unattached, keeps his organs of activity steadfast on the path of God-uniting actions."† A man with such power can instantly fix a new habit in his brain, or stop one at will. An ideal democracy presupposes rational, willing obedience to good laws, without any goading by higher authority or other external influences. Similarly a wise man, one who is really free, avoids error and performs good, not from the compulsion of habit but from free and reasoned choice. Such a one does not permit himself to be dominated by even a good habit, lest in so doing he fail to exercise full discriminative choice of action. A good habit may be in force simply because there has never been any temptation of evil to overthrow it. A good habit thus established is not necessarily fixed permanently in the nature, because it has been maintained not from discriminative choice and reason but as a result of favouring circumstance.

* *Matthew* 13:12.

† Bhagavad Gita III:7.

All national tastes and human customs are habits, circumstantially acquired as a result of environmental influence. Love of Americanism or of Hinduism is the outcome of habit and familiarity. If I had had the choice, I would have preferred to be a human "chameleon," free to embrace the desirable aspects of all nationalities and all creeds.

We can test our power over our habits by commanding the mind to like or dislike a certain food at will. On one occasion I found this particular test useful: Shortly after I had come to America, I attended a dinner at which Roquefort cheese and crackers were served. No sooner had Mr. Roquefort touched the palate, and no sooner had his arrival become known to the cerebral cells, than the habit-lords of taste instituted a rebellion among the honoured guests already gathered in my stomach, who became very upset and began to threaten, "If you let Mr. Roquefort in, we will all leave in a body!" I did not enjoy this sudden embarrassment! Noticing that everyone else at the table was greatly relishing the peculiar food, I strongly urged my senses to elect immediately the Roquefort cheese-enjoying habit. Then I liked the taste at once, and have continued to like it from that time on.

Why is it that you sometimes find yourself acting, or reacting, contrary to your real desires? Because over a period of time you have built up habits that are contrary to those desires, and your actions automatically flatter your habits. You must first establish habits that will influence your actions to cater to your true ideals.

Habit is an automatic mechanism for performing actions without expending the mental and physical labour ordinarily involved in performing actions that are new to us. Wrongly used, this mechanism is an arch-enemy, threatening man's citadel of free choice. Be practical. Try from today to overcome inimical habits hidden within you, garbed as environmental likes and dislikes. Oust them and be free to act from reason alone. Your habits are not you. Shake off that delusion and you will remember your true Self, the perfect image of God within you.

SRI SRI MAHAVATAR BABAJI
Guru of Sri Sri Lahiri Mahasaya

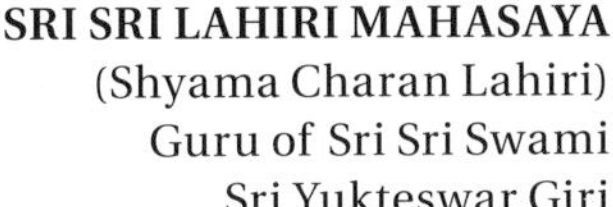

SRI SRI LAHIRI MAHASAYA
(Shyama Charan Lahiri)
Guru of Sri Sri Swami
Sri Yukteswar Giri

SRI SRI SWAMI
SRI YUKTESWAR GIRI
Guru of Sri Sri
Paramahansa Yogananda

DIRECT DISCIPLES OF YOGANANDAJI WHO SUCCEEDED HIM AS SPIRITUAL HEAD OF YSS/SRF

(Left to right) Sri Rajarsi Janakananda, spiritual head and president of Yogoda Satsanga Society of India/Self-Realization Fellowship 1952–1955. Sri Daya Mata succeeded Rajarsi Janakananda in February 1955, serving in these roles for more than 55 years until her passing in 2010. Sri Mrinalini Mata, another close disciple of the great master chosen and trained by him as one of those to lead his work after his passing, fulfilled these responsibilities from early 2011 until her passing in 2017. Sri Swami Chidananda Giri, a YSS/SRF monastic for over 40 years, is the current president and spiritual head of YSS/SRF. For more information on the YSS/SRF lineage please visit our website, www.yssofindia.org.

Self-Analysis: Key to the Mastery of Life

First Self-Realization Fellowship Temple at Encinitas, California, November 6, 1938

Let us leave the confines of ego and wander in the vast fields of soul progress. As time is marching on, so must your souls march on to a greater expansion of your life in Spirit. The initiative to undertake your most important duty in life is often buried beneath the accumulated debris of human habits. You must free yourselves from their stultifying influence and start to sow the seeds of the success that you desire. Life is worthwhile when you are accomplishing the most essential work, which is to find out the meaning and true values of your existence.

Man should be instructed by this cosmic motion picture of life. It is not being shown without a reason. Each day we behold different scenes, and each day has a lesson to teach. You are meant to learn the lesson by concentrating on the supreme purpose of human existence: to know Who is behind your life.

Without Self-Analysis, Man Leads Robotlike Life

Millions of people never analyse themselves. Mentally they are mechanical products of the factory of their environment, preoccupied with breakfast, lunch, and dinner, working and sleeping, and going here and there to be entertained. They don't know what or why they are seeking, nor why they never realise complete happiness and lasting satisfaction. By evading self-analysis, people go on being robots, conditioned by their environment. True self-analysis is the greatest art of progress.

Everyone should learn to analyse himself dispassionately. Write down your thoughts and aspirations daily. Find out what you are—not what you imagine you are!—because you want to make yourself what you ought to be. Most people don't change because they don't see their own faults.

Everyone is the product of his heredity and environment. If you were born in America you reflect distinctive American characteristics. If you were born in China or England, you are likely to reflect the interests of those nationalities. Your environment is the result of your true heredity—the traits and desires acquired by you in past lives. This heredity of past incarnations has led to your being born in the particular family and environment in which you now find yourself.

When we read about the families of important people, we often note that sons of great men are not necessarily of the same mental calibre as their fathers. This failure of biological heredity in man raises a great doubt in our minds: why don't we find the same results in human life that we observe in the plant and animal kingdoms, where good pedigree usually produces good offspring? We must probe the inner life of man for an answer.

Traits from Past Lives Influence Us Now

In a literary family it is not unusual to find a boy who doesn't like literature at all. He has been brought up with literature-loving companions, yet has no affinity for it.

Why? Environment or heredity in the ordinary sense does not explain it. But beyond these factors is reincarnation. We are born into a particular family because of certain characteristics that are similar. But every person in a family is an individual soul who brings his own distinctive traits from his past lives. Hence there are always some biological hereditary resemblances in families, yet each person is different in character.

A man takes birth in a certain family, a particular social and national environment, owing to specific causes—his own past actions. Therefore man is the architect of his own destiny. One can almost predict what he will be in his next life by analysing his dominant interests and habits in this one.

Whatever You Have Done, You Can Undo

So self-analysis is important for the progress of the soul. Let us suppose that tragedies have been your favourite reading for many years, and that you naturally feel you will continue to enjoy them for the rest of your life. But if you analyze yourself and see that you are becoming morose from constant reading of this type of literature, you will wish to form a new habit of perusing inspiring spiritual books. By doing so you will change the course of your life. We can alter ourselves very quickly with strong determination; but without it, one does not change effortlessly or in a minute the habit patterns of years. To eradicate a habit of long standing you must apply the full strength of your determination in counteractivity until the bad habit is worn out. Most persons don't have the necessary patience. But everyone should feel encouraged by this truth: whatever you have created or done, you can undo.

When you analyse what you are, have a firm desire to banish your weaknesses and to make yourself what you ought to be. Don't allow yourself to be overwhelmed with discouragement at the revelation of your shortcomings that honest self-analysis usually brings.

Thought Produces Everything in the Universe

A theory has been advanced that thought is a product of the endocrine glands. Such a conception is unfounded. Flesh cannot produce thought. Mind is the architect of the microcosm and the macrocosm. As water by cooling and condensation becomes ice, so thought by condensation assumes physical form. Everything in the universe is thought in material form. The endocrine organ is just a physical structurisation of a microcosmic thought-blueprint.

The physical and mental aspects of man are closely interrelated; it is commonly observed that a person whose liver is out of order becomes cranky. When you are bilious, you don't feel like smiling and saying "Peace" to everyone! You feel unamiable. Your thoughts and emotions are affected by your physical state.

A weakening of the organs has a corresponding weakening effect on mental power. Those who eat a great deal of meat are often surly and full of vexation. If I were to put you on a grape-juice diet for a week, it is likely you would feel uplifted and harmoniously disposed toward all.*

* Overeating and improper eating create in the body excessive toxins that have a definite negative effect on the mind, making it both sluggish and irritable. Occasional fasting on grape or orange juice has a cleansing effect on the system, which in turn vitalizes the brain. Such fasts, undertaken one day a week, or occasionally for three days at a time, have been found effective in helping to keep the body properly cleansed of impurities. Fasting for longer than three days at a time should be under the supervision of someone well trained in the science of fasting.

I recently met a man who was wearing just a lightweight suit and no overcoat, although it was terribly cold. He said he was seventy years old, and that he never feels cold. He didn't even wear socks! He had accustomed his body to chilly weather. Mind influences body more than vice versa, but the bodily chemicals do exercise a constant influence on the mind.* Body and mind are interdependent.

Dreams Reveal the Omnipotence of Mind

For example, suppose I am dreaming that I am awake and in the kitchen, and very hungry. I eat something and drink a glass of milk. My hunger and thirst are gone, and I feel satisfied. What was the cause of my satisfaction? Was it the food? Remember, I am dreaming. Is it not simply a change of thought that made me feel satisfied? Since I am dreaming, it is my mind that thought it had taken food. The hunger and the food and the milk were only ideas in my dream. All were made of the same mind-stuff. When I wake up I realise that my experiences were nothing but a series of ideas. A mere change of thought removed the unpleasant sensation of hunger and substituted the pleasant sensation of eating food and drinking milk. So you see, thought by itself can do anything.

Once I was travelling by train when the weather was extremely hot; the air felt as if it were coming from a furnace. Everyone around me was suffering, but I was

* Serious research on the effect of diet and nutrition on mental health was begun many years after Paramahansa Yogananda had made this observation. Persons from poverty areas who were denied proper nourishment showed decidedly slower mental development and responses. In addition, science has shown that some forms of insanity (heretofore considered incurable) improved remarkably with the simple administration of vitamins, and that the causes of certain forms of depression, anxiety, and other emotions can be traced to chemical imbalances in the system. *(Publisher's Note)*

smiling within because my mind was dissociated from the thought of the heat. I had said to myself: "Lord, the same electricity that makes heat in a furnace makes ice in a refrigerator. Therefore why shouldn't I be able to redirect that electricity of Yours to produce cold right now?" In that instant I felt as if a sheet of ice had enveloped me.

Change Your Mental Attitude

We should bear in mind, however, that it is not wise to disregard the body wholly. One should eat proper foods in preference to wrong foods. And if you must live with people who make you nervous, then once in a while you should change your surroundings. But it is better still if you can change your *mental* environment, so that you won't be disturbed by others' actions. Change yourself, and you can then live anywhere in peace and happiness.

Most of the world is like a mental hospital. Some people are sick with jealousy, others with anger, hatred, passion. They are victims of their habits and emotions. But you can make your home a place of peace. Analyse yourself. All emotions are reflected in the body and mind. Envy and fear cause the face to pale, and love makes it glow. Learn to be calm and you will always be happy.

So remember, whatever type of ego you have, whatever personality you are trying to express, you should make an effort to analyse your true nature and to develop its best qualities. One may have a moral ego or a patriotic ego or an artistic ego or a businessman's ego, and so on. If morality is your ideal, live uprightly and express your goodwill to all. That is real morality. It is pride that makes self-righteous persons so ready to judge those about them who are weak. True morality includes compassion for others in their ignorant wrongdoings.

Those who are products of the material ego suffer much and needlessly. Such persons should learn self-control; otherwise they are just like pieces of matter in action—they have to smoke so many times a day, they must eat certain foods, they always get a headache if they miss their lunch, they can sleep only in a particular kind of bed. It is all right to utilise creature comforts, but never be enslaved by them.

If you are a cross between an intellectual and a materialistic ego, that is better. But unless you develop and maintain a balanced nature—intellectually, materially, and spiritually—you are not going to be happy. Your spiritual intuition tells you how to control your life, so that you are not mastered by it. It is unwise to let the materialistic ego govern your judgement; your conscience and intuition should decide.

The Conditions of Happiness: Plain Living, High Thinking

Plain living and high thinking should be your goal. Learn to carry all the conditions of happiness within yourself by meditating and attuning your consciousness to the ever-existing, ever-conscious, ever-new Joy, which is God. Your happiness should never be subject to any outside influence. Whatever your environment is, don't allow your inner peace to be touched by it. Analyze yourself; make yourself what you should be and what you want to be. People seldom learn true self-control; they do things that are detrimental to their highest welfare and think they are making themselves happy; but they are not. To be able to do things when and because you ought to do them, and to refrain from doing what you know is injurious—these are keys to real success and happiness.

Don't keep your mind engaged in too many activities. Analyze what you get from them, and see if they are really important. Don't waste your time. To read a good book improves you much more than seeing movies. I often say, "If you read for one hour, write in your spiritual diary for two hours; and if you write for two hours, think for three hours; and if you think for three hours, meditate all the time." No matter where I go, I keep my mind continuously on my soul peace. You too should always point the needle of your attention toward the North Pole of spiritual joy. Then no one can ever disturb your equilibrium.

Remember, if each day does not find you a better person than you were the day before, you are going backward—in health, in mental peace, and in soul joy. Why? Because you don't exercise enough control over your actions. You yourself made your habits, and you can change them. If you have been thinking wrongly, make up your mind to be with good company and to study and meditate. A change of company can make a great difference to you. When you come here, even for these few hours, your mentality changes; you feel a refreshing peace. When you go to a dance or a party your mind is often restless, nervous, and excited. Afterward, if you enter a different, calmer atmosphere, you feel more peaceful again. The greatest influence in your life, stronger even than your will power, is your environment. Change that, if necessary. Until you are mentally strong, you can never be what you want to be without a good environment to help you. When you are having difficulty in trying to change for the better, spiritual company and other uplifting influences are essential.

Self-analysis is also essential to help you better yourself. If you can analyze yourself fearlessly, you will be able to stand the critical analysis of others without flinching.

Those who like to dwell on the faults of others are human vultures. There is already too much evil in the world. Don't talk of evil, don't think of evil, and don't do evil. Be like a rose, wafting to all the sweet fragrance of soul goodness. Make everyone feel that you are a friend; that you are a helper, not a destroyer. If you want to be good, analyse yourself and develop the virtues in you. Banish the thought that evil has any part in your nature, and it will drop off. Make everyone else feel that you are an image of God, not by your words but by your behaviour. Emphasise the light, and darkness will be no more. Study, meditate, and do good to others.

Seclusion Is the Price of Greatness

Seclusion is the price of greatness. Be alone within. Don't lead the aimless life that so many persons follow. Meditate and read good books more. There are so many inspiring things to know, and yet man spends his time foolishly. Happiness will never come if you don't concentrate and act on the wisdom of great men. Their thoughts are there to help you, in the scriptures and other truthful books.

So don't waste time, constantly seeking new excitement. Once in a while it is all right to go to the movies and have a little social life, but mostly remain apart and live within yourself. Happiness depends on meditation, on knowing great minds through their thoughts in books, and on surrounding yourself with people who are noble and kind. Enjoy solitude; but when you want to mix with others, do so with all your love and friendship, so that those persons cannot forget you, but remember always that they met someone who inspired them and turned their minds toward God.

Man's Eternal Quest

First Self-Realization Fellowship Temple at Encinitas, California, February 16, 1941

The flowers outside* are so beautiful, but behind them is a garden still more lovely. Though it is very subtle and hard to discern in the beginning, if you can penetrate to the inner realm through the door of the spiritual eye† you will discover it. I live in that garden—a region of exquisite qualities, of tender thoughts more sweet and fragrant than any flower. There the bee of my mind is continuously drinking the honey of God's presence.

As we interiorise our concentration and live more and more in that invisible land within us, we find that our soul qualities take special forms; each materialisation is a window through which we perceive the Lord's indescribable sweetness. Don't think that the search for God consists only in meditation. Every good quality that you express in thought and action yields the hidden nectar of God's presence, if your inner perception is deep enough.

When we pass through the door of the spiritual eye, we see inside ourselves the factory of intelligent Life Energy that has created the whole universe. Because we don't concentrate within, we are mystified by the

* Colourful gardens surrounded the first Self-Realization Fellowship Golden Lotus Temple in Encinitas.

† Through the "single eye" within the centre of the forehead, man can behold the inner astral and causal worlds behind the gross physical cosmos.

imprints of the invisible Spirit in nature. We behold the productions of God; His name is written in the flower and in the sky, in everything—but He is silent. As human beings we are very much privileged, for among all God's creatures man alone has the physical, mental, and spiritual endowment necessary to seek Him, to find Him, to know Him, and to understand His language of silence.

What Is a Successful Life?

A child pictures success as having all kinds of playthings, and perhaps a toy car to ride in. A poor child thinks how happy he would be if only he had a lot of toys. A wealthy child, on the other hand, may be bored with his playthings; he has a restlessness in his soul. In time it may become very difficult to please the child of the rich, for he already has so many possessions. When we are older, we laugh at the desires of our childhood; and who knows but that whatever we are wishing for now, thinking it will bring the fulfilment of our life's dream, will one day have little significance for us? I found this to be so. I didn't want to become drunk with emotions, heedlessly bent on the follies I saw others pursuing, and I looked farther on. If we gaze a little ahead we can see for ourselves that most of the things we think we want are not going to make us really happy.

Success is necessary in order to possess the essentials of life: food, clothing, shelter, and health. If you don't have these to at least a certain degree, you are in a wretched position. You should be able to attain the minimum amount of comfort and happiness that you are seeking. Whether one is a spiritual or a material idealist, all persons can agree that there are a few basic physical needs that must be met so that man can preserve his bodily temple. Unless he maintains this temple, he cannot succeed in anything else.

Happiness Is a Creation of Our Own Mind

But what is real success? If you attained everything you wanted in this life, you would eventually become disillusioned anyway. By analyzing I saw for myself that the only pleasure I had in anything was that which my mind gave to it. If I withdrew my attention, enjoyment of any object vanished. Thus I saw that pleasure is internal, a concept of one's own mind. The beauty of your most valued possession, which you may be holding in front of your eyes, disappears when your thoughts are absent from it. Only when you put your mind on it do you perceive its loveliness. Therefore it is reasonable to say that within us, and not outside us, lies most of the happiness we are seeking.

We can magnify our happiness or minimise it. One person has a little home and says, "I enjoy it more than a palace." Someone else has a palace in which he does not take as much pleasure as the other person has in his unpretentious cottage. The secret of success and happiness is inside you. If you have found success and prosperity outside, but not inside, you are not truly successful. A millionaire who is not happy is not successful. I don't mean that if you have a million dollars you cannot be a success. Whether you are rich or poor, if you get happiness out of life you are a real success.

Pleasure that lasts only for a moment and leaves you with regret afterward is not happiness. In true success, even though the first excitement of delight in some accomplishment fades away, the gratifying memory of fulfilment remains. All the good things that you have done in your life stay on in your memory as a joy forever. They are the real success that you have attained.

To Be Happy Under All Circumstances Is Real Success

Success is not a simple matter; it cannot be determined merely by the amount of money and material possessions you have. The meaning of success goes far deeper. It can only be measured by the extent to which your inner peace and mental control enable you to be happy under all circumstances. That is real success. When you can look within and your conscience is clear, your reason unprejudiced, your will firm yet flexible, and your discrimination strong; and when you are able to obtain at will the things you need and the things you consider worthwhile, you are a success.

As a child you could be happy with little things, but now you tend to think you have to own several homes and cars, even though you can see that those who have them are not invariably happy. Plain living and high thinking make for contentment. Keeping your mind on the plane of ideas will give you more happiness than if you dwell on externals. Those who are preoccupied mostly with looking after their home, their possessions, their dress, are not necessarily civilised. You can dress up a dog, but that doesn't make it civilised. The difference between man and the dog is that man can voluntarily change his consciousness and his nature. He can penetrate deep within, into the region of the Spirit, where the dog cannot. Man's love is transcendental. When we die, the dog may grieve for us a little while, in some cases till death, but human friends never forget us (if they don't want to!) throughout incarnations. So mankind has tremendous advantages over other creatures.

Evolutionary Human Progress Lies in the Power of Thought

As a human being, you make your greatest evolutionary progress by the power of thought. Set aside some time each day to improve your mind. It is more commendable to read awhile than to occupy yourself day and night with housework or with noncreative activities. Plan your life so that you do not live in a haphazard way; but if your tendency is to overorganise your time, get away from that extreme also. Balance is necessary in every avenue of life. Instead of using your mind only to plan your everyday work and other passing activities, or with idle mind letting your time slip away, employ it some of the time in constructive reading. Have at hand some worthwhile reading material, and peruse it during free moments. It is more effective to have a variety of literature—a bit of science, a bit of history, philosophy, biography, travel—anything that will expand and inspire your mind.

Books can be dear friends, and if your selections are choice ones you will experience much benefit from them. It may seem very hard at first when you read Emerson or Milton or Plato, or some of the great saints, but after a while you will find yourself thinking about what they have written. You will feel you have gained something, because all those sages received their wisdom from the infinite treasure-house of God—ideas that otherwise might not occur to you in a lifetime.

However, many people read constantly and yet cannot tell you what they have read. The best way to read a book is to introspect about it. See how it applies to your own life. And learn to discriminate. Do not accept blindly everything that you read; it should meet the tests of your mind. To be worthwhile, books should cause you to think. If they do that, you will find that your mind is developing.

Receive Knowledge Directly from Spirit

People who do not read or meditate, who live only externally, do not develop any deep understanding. Meditation keeps you directly in tune with the Power that evokes all thought. To touch that Supreme Power is meditation. As a human being you do injustice to yourself if you don't read; but to meditate is still better. I would like to read, but I can scarcely finish two pages before I am called to attend to something else, so I have given up reading. I find it more profitable to meditate. As I go deep within, radiant lights appear and great joy comes, joy that remains with me all day long. Such is my experience. Such is the experience of all who commune with the ever blissful Lord.

Don't waste your time. God wants you to be a balanced individual. If you allow your life to become unbalanced you will be punished by the cosmic law. Live simply, have daily physical exercise, study rewarding books, and cultivate the habit of daily meditation. If you meditate you will find much more happiness than you have ever known. All knowledge will be given to you from within.

My life has been that way. I have not read twenty books since I came to America twenty years ago. I am not proud of the fact; I would have been wholly ignorant if I hadn't had, through meditation, the consciousness of Spirit. When I look at a book I see that whatever truth it contains has already been given to me from God. All thought and truth come from Spirit; if you commune with Him you receive His wisdom direct. So, read good books rather than waste time on unproductive activities; but better still, meditate and anchor your mind on the ultimate Truth, which is God.

Man's Evolution Ordained by Cosmic Law

In different ages and places, man has developed, by his thought processes, various ideas about life and the soul. For instance, when members of some primitive tribes have headaches, they think their soul is lost, and they appeal to the medicine man for healing. He goes out in the woods looking for the lost soul, which he brings back in a box. Then he "replaces" the "soul" in the patient's head, and the headache is supposed to go away. It is the custom in another culture, when anyone is sick, to put fishhooks into his flesh so that if he happens to sneeze, his soul will not escape but will be caught by the hooks.

As through the process of faulty thought some people have arrived at erroneous conclusions about the soul, so by true reasoning others have come to a more profound understanding. We know that the soul is not a puff of breath, because there are persons who have lived long in the suspended-animation state without breathing at all, showing that the soul cannot be bound by breath. The soul is something beyond breath or any other physical condition.

Whether or not one believes in himself as a soul, he is bound by the cosmic law to develop, consciously or unconsciously, his deeper nature. Whatever a person's occupation in life, his consciousness is evolving whenever he is planning something or otherwise using his intelligence creatively. Man evolves through every constructive action he performs.

The trouble with most people is that when they are performing an action they are thinking about something else. They don't know how to concentrate on what they are doing when they are doing it. You should learn to think of one thing at a time with all the power of your mind. Your whole attention should be there. Don't drag along. Doing things in a lackadaisical way leads to failure and misery.

Man should not be a psychological automaton, like the animal, which acts only through instinct. To be unthinking is a great sin against Spirit, which abides in you; we are meant to be conscious of what we do. We should reflect before we act. We should learn how to use our minds so that we can evolve and realise our oneness with the Creator. Everything we do should be the result of premeditated thought.

Aim for high goals. It is a waste to use the power of thought to obtain things that are not important. Learn to remove the weeds that have grown in the garden of the mind. Make your mental garden so beautiful that God will come there. If you want to have such a mental garden, blooming in the soil of wisdom, you must make your life simple. By doing everything consciously, not absentmindedly, you can analyze your activities; then choose what is important and cut out the nonessentials. As soon as you are through with your duties, withdraw your mind from them and employ it in other creative pursuits.

God Fulfils Man's Eternal Quest

Learn how to cultivate the consciousness of Spirit. That is why you were born a human being. You were created under the evolutionary law that you might exercise your divine powers to find God. The animal can't find

Him. Lahiri Mahasaya was working on the science of helping animals to evolve more quickly; but he didn't live to finish this work. I, also, know of some ways to quicken the evolution of the lower forms of life. But what of the millions of human beings who are living like animals? When they leave this world they haven't fulfilled the purpose of their existence. Why not fulfil it now? You can if you concentrate. The only meaning of life is to find the all-loving God, who has kept us apart from Himself by shyly hiding from us. We must find Him. Mankind is engaged in an eternal quest for that "something else" he hopes will bring him happiness, complete and unending. For those individual souls who have sought and found God, the search is over: He is that Something Else.

Nature Veils God's Presence

Why was temptation given to man? That he might look for the One who is more tempting than any worldly temptation. The earthly lures that surround you are not intended to ensnare you, but to cause you to seek beyond them; to make you ask, "Who created all these things? Who made me? Who am I? Where are You, Lord? Why are You hiding? Talk to me!" When you directly approach God with these questions, He answers. Most people don't call deeply enough to Him, and so they never find Him. You must speak clearly to Him in the language of your soul: "Lord, I want no longer to see only the beauty You have created. I want to behold Your Face, which is more beautiful than the flowers, more entrancing than all other faces. I want to see Who is behind all nature." Even if a person covers himself with a veil you can see that someone is there. So is nature like a great veil bulging with God's presence. He is hiding there, but you take just a casual look, not penetrating to see the shy Indweller. As I sit breathless, silent, watchful in meditation, I become aware of a blissful trembling stir within me, and He whispers: "I am here."

The intelligence God has given us is the gateway to Heaven. It is the outer door to His kingdom, but you don't use it. Why not use it now, today? Don't wait, only to leave the earth like a dog, kicked out by death. It is a crime against your soul. Your intelligence was given to you to discover why you were placed here: to find Him.

How to Discover Spirit

There are various techniques for discovering the Spirit. Silence is one of them. Practising silence means to silence all desires that try to percolate into your consciousness from outside, so you can go deeper within to feel your soul.

Another step or technique is devotion, or speaking to God purely and simply: "You have created me. I didn't want to be created. It is Your responsibility to reveal Yourself to me." Talking to Him a little while and then forgetting will never bring His response. God is "hard to get" because not everyone "means business" with Him. The technique of prayer is usually ineffectual because most prayers are not deep or devotional enough. You have to repeat and repeat until you go really deep, into the superconsciousness. Prayer in which your very soul is burning with desire for God is the only effectual prayer. You have prayed like that at some time, no doubt; perhaps when you wanted something very badly, or urgently needed money —then you burned up the ether with your desire. That is how you must feel for God. Talk to Him day and night; you will see that He will respond.

Yoga Is the Science of Finding God

The Yoga system of contacting God is the best. It consists of various scientifically effective techniques of meditation. The great sages of India reasoned that logically there must be an exact law by which to approach God, just as there are exact laws by which He operates His universes. Through their experiments, the spiritual laws of yoga were discovered. The science of yoga will take hold in this country more than any other form of spiritual seeking. The entire trend will be away from churches, where people go only to hear a sermon, and into schools and quiet places where they will go to meditate and really find God.

Everyone should practise divine communion with God. This is what Jesus did when he was with his disciples. I am not here just to tell you about the sugar of God's presence; my greatest aim is to make sure you taste it. What is the use of my talking about God unless you know Him and taste His sweetness? You must realise God, as I have realised Him.

It is not out of pride that I speak this way, but because I am sent here to testify to you about Him. Day and night I think about my Lord. I am not wasting my time. Everything I do I am doing only for Him, so engrossed that I don't notice the passage of time or feel fatigue from my daily activities. I feel His presence when I work. That is also my meditation. I often give this illustration: Some worldly men remain drunk for years by hiding now and then to take a little drink to sustain the euphoric feeling; then they go back to their work. So is the divine man; he hides from people and meditates upon the Lord. Drinking deep of the intoxicating wine of God's presence, he whispers, "Lord, You are so wonderful, so marvellous! I love You." Then he goes back to his duties. Inwardly he talks to God all the time, no matter what he is doing.

I am never separated from Him for a second. That is the state I wanted and worked for. I remember that once in a while I used to feel that He had gone away from me, and at such time I wanted to die rather than live without Him. I didn't find happiness in anything. Thus does the lover of God suffer when separated from Him. But a time comes when the devotee beholds the Lord dancing everywhere, and feels the immortal fountain of His spirit and His bliss ever bubbling in his soul. This what you will feel if you meditate. Pray with such intensity that He will come to you. In the Gita is a beautiful promise from the Lord: "Immerse thy mind in Me alone; concentrate on Me thy discriminative perception; and beyond doubt thou shalt dwell immortally in Me."*

The yoga techniques are more scientific than prayer; that is why they lead more swiftly to divine communion. In my youth, when I sought Him with prayer alone, it often took a long time to get results. After I had learned Kriya Yoga and practised it, with deep devotion, I achieved results in a few minutes. Krishna taught that yoga meditation is greater than the path of asceticism, the path of devotion or prayer, the path of right action, or the path of discrimination.† It is a faster way. An airplane will take you from Los Angeles to new York in a matter of hours; by bullock cart the journey would last several months. If you practise yoga, you will find it to be the airplane of spiritual progress.

* Bhagavad Gita XII:8.

† Bhagavad Gita VI:46.

After you have perfected yourself in the Yoga path, which embraces bodily discipline, mental discipline, and spiritual discipline, the obstacles to spiritual success are overcome and you can commune freely with God. That is why it is the highest path. And that is why I am trying to acquaint people with it. Yoga is not a myth, a creation of someone's imagination. It is a true science.

Why shouldn't you take from India the greatest methods for finding God that have ever been given to mankind? I went to the masters in India for training, and they taught me about Christ in a profound and loving way such as never I heard in the West. I saw Christ in their company. They talked with him. Did St. Francis lie to us? He saw Christ every night. Lord Jesus lives! I have seen him. When you are behind a screen you see everyone else outside, but they can't see you. So the saints and the angels can see you, but you can't see them unless you practise yoga.*

Your Prayer Must Be Intense to Reach God

Last summer I stopped at a monastery, where I met one of the priests. He was a wonderful soul. I asked him how long he had been on the spiritual path as a monk.

"About twenty-five years," he replied. Then I asked:

"Do you see Christ?"

"I don't deserve it," he answered. "Maybe after death he will visit me."

* There have been mystics of various faiths who, through their transcendent powers of devotion to God, have attained to the breathless state of superconscious ecstasy that alone brings true inner vision. The spiritual fervour of such great souls is beyond the emotional scope of the average person. For mankind as a whole, the only hope of divine illumination lies in the yogic approach to God through daily practise of scientific spiritual methods.

"No," I assured him, "you can see him from tonight if you make up your mind." Tears were in his eyes, and he remained silent.

You must pray intensely. If you sit night after night practising meditation and crying to God, the darkness will be burned up, and you will see the Light behind this physical light, the Life behind all life, the Father behind all fathers, the Mother behind all mothers, the Friend behind all friends, the Element behind all elements, the Power behind all powers. That is where I live, and where I want you to come.

Practising of Yoga Awakens Soul Longing

You have gone away from God like the prodigal son, and it is only by returning to Him, within, that you will make this vale of tears a haven of heaven. There is no other way. If everyone in this world were a millionaire there would still be troubles and sorrows, for you cannot buy unshakable happiness. That comes only by following a technique of yoga, and by devotion, by going within. Practising yoga is half the battle. Even if you don't feel enthusiastic in the beginning, if you go on practising you will come to feel that tremendous longing for God which is necessary if you are to find Him.

Why don't you make the effort? Whence do all the beautiful things in creation continually emerge? Whence comes the intelligence of great souls, but from the storehouse of the Infinite Spirit? And if these wonders you see about you are not enough to induce you to seek Him, why should He reveal Himself to you? He has given you the capacity for love that you may yearn for Him above all else. Don't misuse your love and reason. And don't misuse your concentration and intelligence on false goals.

This World Is Only Pictures of Light

Night is the time for meditation; never go to bed until you have communion. I never do. Last night as I sat on my bed His presence engulfed me. The whole room and everything in it was blinding Light. Even when I slept I remained locked in the arms of the Divine. Never have I felt such joy.

This world is all a motion-picture projection of God's mind. There is no death, no disease, no wickedness. Someday, when He will show you His Light transforming itself into this terrible cosmic motion picture of life and death, and then withdraw the picture so that only His Light remains, you can laugh at the unreality of His light-and-shadow creation. You will know then that He has created everything out of His Light; and that only the Light is real. We must fully shake ourselves out of this dream delusion to realise that we are rays of that immortal Light. This realization comes with the practice of the highest yoga technique of meditation. It cannot be conveyed in lectures.

God Is Our Only True Goal

Every now and then I receive a letter from the Self-Realization students in London. During these terrible air raids they have not missed one Self-Realization Fellowship service. That is the real spirit of England and that is the spirit that will save England. Politicians can never save the world; it is only understanding God that will save the world. He is our true goal in this life. Otherwise there would be no incentive for going on.

Those who love God should worship Him in all religions. "In whatever way people are devoted to Me, in that measure (according to their desire, their degree of understanding, and their manner of worship) I manifest Myself to them. All men, regardless of their mode of seeking, pursue a path to Me."* Criticise no one's faith. There should be a genuine feeling of love and respect for all. Wherever you see a temple or church you should inwardly bow down to the Spirit there. It is not for everyone to be a teacher, but you can always draw the attention of others to spiritual things. Don't waste your time, spending hours listening to the radio and reading useless novels. Be entertained by the divine messages coming from your own soul. Just by a gentle attuning touch of my love, I hear His programme here in my heart.

No one can bring you salvation unless you earn it—not through belief, not through following dogma, but by your own knowledge and experience. You should ask yourself these questions every day: If there is a God, why don't I see Him? If there are saints, where are they? The answers will be given to you; you can commune with God and His saints if you practise the science of Kriya Yoga. My sole desire is to give you the Truth, that you may experience what I experience.

The purpose of this life is to find your Self. Know your Self. Feel the throb of the ocean of God's presence in your heart. Suppose you are floating in the ocean, rocked on the bosom of its might vastness, and when you swim ashore, you still feel the whole ocean, surging behind you as you walk onto the beach—this is the way I feel God. He never leaves any of His children for a moment. He will reply to all your questions, and then there will be no more fears.

Find that Power, feel the ocean of His love behind your consciousness, and you will achieve the greatest success man can attain.

* Bhagavad Gita IV:11.

The Desire That Satisfies All Desires

Self-Realization Fellowship International Headquarters, Los Angeles, California, October 26, 1939

The glory of God is great. He is real, and He can be found in this life. In men's hearts there are many prayers—for money, fame, health—prayers for all manner of things. But the prayer that should be first in every heart is the prayer for God's presence. Silently and surely, as you walk on the path of life, you must come to the realization that God is the only object, the only goal that will satisfy you; for in God lies the answer to every desire of the heart.

When you have found it impossible to fulfil some urgent wish by your own effort, you turn to God in prayer. Thus every prayer that you utter represents a desire. But when you find God, all desires vanish, and there is no need for prayer. I don't pray. That may seem a strange thing to say, but when the Object of your prayer is with you all the time, you no longer have need to pray. In fulfilment of the wish or prayer for Him lies joy eternal.

Material desires come through certain mistaken conceptions about the purpose of life. This earth is not our home. The scriptures have told us we are children of God, made in His image, and that it is the will of the Divine that we return to our Source. What man does not realise is that unless and until he goes back to the Source, back to God, he will have to struggle to fulfil endless desires. Reflect on that. Man cannot help having desires, and it is not a sin to have them; but most human longings hamper fulfilment of the supreme desire to return to God, hence they are detrimental to man's happiness. Until he wants and has God, man will continue to long for whatever else he believes will make him happy. But to him who has God, instant fulfilment of all desires comes automatically.

There are two classes of desires: those that help us to find God, and those that obstruct our finding Him. For example, if someone hits you, you want to retaliate; but if you overcome that desire by using the superior power of love, you have applied the action that will help you to find God. All desires should be satisfied in the divine way. When you try to satisfy them in the worldly way, you only multiply your difficulties. If you learn to give every desire to God, He will see to it that your good desires are fulfilled and the harmful ones are overcome. There is no protection greater than your conscience, and the divine quality of your good desires. If you but looked at your soul, the all-perfect reflection of God within you, you would find all your desires satisfied! In that divine consciousness, having which, no other gain is greater, you would be unmoved even if the whole world were given to you; neither would praise elate you, nor blame hurt. You would feel only the great joy of God within.

God's Children Should Not Beg

Always seek the guidance of the Divine in trying to fulfil your legitimate desires, because that is the supreme way to receive the answers to all your prayers. But one thing you must remember: cut out begging from your prayer! Change your old attitude of supplication. You should pray to God intimately, as His child, which you are. God does not object when you pray from your ego,* as a stranger and a beggar, but you will find that your efforts are limited by that consciousness. God does not want you to give up your own will power, which is your divine birthright as His child.

Naturally, one should distinguish between reasonable and unreasonable prayers or desires. And bear in mind that, once you have made this discrimination, whatever good or bad desires you hold on to are bound to be fulfilled. If you cling to any evil desires, they will be granted; and you will find out what harm and unhappiness they cause. As time goes on, you will realise that even though your wish was fulfilled, your heart is still not satisfied; you will feel something within you rebelling. For example, suppose you have weak digestion, yet you want to eat fried foods. Not surprisingly, you suffer every time you do. Although you feel delight while fulfilling that desire, the after-effect is pain; thus you are made aware that you have done wrong. It is wiser to use discrimination to separate your evil desires from your good ones and, having done so, to avoid the fulfilment of those wrong desires. Learn to be guided by your conscience, the divine discriminative power within you.

The Danger of Unfulfilled Desires

Unfulfilled desires remain in the heart. And what is the harm in harbouring them? It is this: Every desire consists of specific forces, either good or evil, or a mixture of both. And when you die, though your body is gone, those forces do not die. As mental tabloids they follow your soul wherever it goes, and when you are reborn, these tabloids manifest as behavioural tendencies. Thus, a person who has died an alcoholic brings with him the tendency to

* The ego consciousness; identification with the mortal body, which creates a feeling of separateness from God, and hence a feeling of limitation.

alcoholism when he is reborn; and it remains with him until he overcomes desire for alcohol.

The behaviour of even the smallest child reveals certain characteristics of past lives. Some children have terrible temper tantrums; others are moody. God did not make them that way. Unfulfilled desires of past lives fashioned those psychological tendencies; and, because of them, the soul, even though made in the image of God, appears as something different. If the image of God within you is distorted in this life by anger or fear, and you do not conquer such uncharacteristic qualities now, you will be reborn with them; and you will have the burden of these misery-creating tendencies until you overcome them in some future incarnation.

It is better, therefore, to work out or overcome all your desires now. They would be finished immediately and for all time in the supreme joy of God's presence; but until you know Him, your unconquered desires will remain to hound you.

There are two ways of finishing your desires—by realising, through reason and discrimination, or wisdom, that only God can give permanent unalloyed happiness; and by fulfilment. In many cases desires lie hidden within the subconscious. You think they are finished, but they are not. Life is indeed a great mystery; but the mystery clears away when you dissect life with the scalpel of reason. If every day you sit quietly for a little while and analyze yourself, you will discover that you have many unsatisfied desires. They are like dangerous germs that you carry through life, and wherever you go, in this life or the next, they will go with you.

The best course is to do away with all dangerous desires in this life, by discrimination, and to concentrate on fulfilling your good desires. If you feel drawn to commit suicide, or to do something evil, get rid of such desires now. Convince yourself, by reason and by good actions, that you are a child of God, made in His image, and rise above your moods and bodily habits. Be more detached. In this way you will conquer. If you suffer from a chronic ailment, try mentally to separate yourself from the consciousness of the body. By discrimination you can conquer the senses. Discrimination is the fire that burns up desire.

It is a general practice to store in the attic all of one's unwanted, unnecessary "junk," and once in a while to have a good house-cleaning. Similarly, hidden away in the attic of your subconscious mind are many potentially harmful desires that one day may give you great trouble. It is important, therefore, to analyze yourself. Perhaps you are a hateful or moody or angry type of person. If so, these stored traits are the result of your own past behaviour. In order to clean out your mental attic of such unwanted furnishings, you must vigorously employ constructive, positive, loving action.

Love Thine Enemies

Suppose that even though an old enemy dies, you continue to feel hatred toward him. In time that bitterness will produce ill effects in your own body and mind. It is better to concentrate on trying to behold God in your enemy; for by doing so you release yourself from evil vengeful desires that destroy your peace of mind. By heaping hatred upon hatred, or giving hate in return for hate, you not only increase your enemy's hostility toward you; you poison your system, physically as well as emotionally, with your own venom.

Conscience Will Tell You What You Are

Sometimes one feels a desire to "take it easy." This is not wrong; to get away from everything now and then gives a person a chance to think what life is all about. Most people are floating along on the current of custom and fashion. They have never actually lived their own life; they have lived the life of the world, and where has it gotten them? So it is wise now and then to remove yourself from everyday considerations; to calm your mind and try to understand what kind of person you are and what kind of person you want to be. And remember, the truest testimony you can find is the testimony of your own conscience, the discriminative voice of the soul. Whatever your conscience says, that is what you are. Think of the power of the conscience of Jesus. His accusers spat upon him and crucified him and yet he said, "Father, forgive them." That kind of discrimination is the only power that will bring light on your path. Whenever there is an overwhelming desire in your heart to pray for a certain thing, use your discrimination. Ask yourself, "Is it a good desire or a bad desire for which I seek fulfilment?"

Man's Lost Treasure Is God

There are many influences that nourish desires in you. When you see a new model car, you want one. When you see a new model house, you want one. Some new style of apparel comes out and immediately you yearn to wear that fashion. Whence do these desires come? I used to sit for hours pondering this. Can you classify all your desires? I sorted mine, and kept only the good ones; and when I had the contact of God, I found all those good desires at once fulfilled. Today you wish for one thing and tomorrow you hanker after something else. Your mind, having descended from almighty God, is not satisfied with the offerings of this world; and it will never be satisfied, because you have lost your soul's richest treasure, which alone can satisfy all your desires, and that is God.

It is true there are some good and necessary desires, and you should strive to fulfil them. But never forget, while pursuing your little desires, to satisfy first your supreme desire—for God. Belief in the necessity of fulfilling lesser desires and duties first is man's greatest delusion. I well remember that during my training as a young disciple of my guru, Swami Sri Yukteswarji, I kept promising myself daily, "I will meditate longer tomorrow." A whole year slipped by before I realised that I was still putting it off. At once I made a resolution that first thing in the morning I would clean my body and then meditate long. But even then, as soon as I stirred about I became caught up in my daily duties and activities. Thereupon I resolved to have my meditation first. Thus I learned a great lesson: First comes my duty to God, and then I take care of all lesser duties. Why not? God says, "Why should I open the doors of eternity to you, when you put other duties before Me?" If you are not soaring to the heights of Spirit, of what account are you? You have nothing to offer God or man.

So seek Him first. To give more importance to your earthly duties is false reasoning, because at any moment the angel Gabriel may call you—at any moment you may be taken away from here. Why then give so much importance to life? for life is very peculiar. You think you are quite secure. Suddenly a loved one dies, or you lose your health, and all security vanishes. How I loved my mother and thought she would be with me always, and suddenly

I found she was gone!* Don't be afraid of death, but be prepared for it.

Life is not what it seems to be. Don't trust it, for it is very tricky, and full of disappointments. Perfection was not meant to be found here. I am not giving you a false picture of life. This is not the kingdom of God; it is God's laboratory, where He is testing souls to see if they will overcome evil desires by good ones, and make Him their supreme desire, so they can return home to His kingdom.

Take God, Not Life, Seriously

Life is full of tragedy and comedy, a kaleidoscope of infinite variety. No two things are the same. Everyone's life is individual. Each person has a different kind of face, a different kind of mind and desires. We would become bored if we had exactly the same experiences every day; we would soon tire of life. Were heaven itself the same every day, we wouldn't want it . We enjoy variety. The stereotyped conception of heaven is all wrong. If it were boring, all the saints would pray to come back to earth for a little change! Heaven is something infinitely different, ever pleasantly new, whereas earth is often unpleasantly new!

Yet, no matter how trying life is, most people become accustomed to it and assume there is no other way to live. Not being able to compare this life with the spiritual life, they do not realise how painful and boring earthly living is.

Actually, life is not real; it is only an entertainment. And just as old movies are shown over and over, so basically the same old incidents occur and recur in life. And although life will go on eternally, the same themes depicted

* Paramahansa Yogananda was not yet eleven when his mother died. *(Publisher's Note)*

in past films will be portrayed again and again. It is true that history repeats itself. We are all museum pieces!

Whatever comes in life, just take it joyfully, impersonally, as you would a motion picture. Life is entertaining when we do not take it too seriously. A good laugh is an excellent remedy for human ills. One of the best characteristics of the American people is their ability to laugh. To be able to laugh at life is marvellous. This my master [Swami Sri Yukteswar] taught me. In the beginning of my training in his hermitage, I went about with a solemn face, never smiling. One day Master pointedly remarked, "What is this? Are you attending a funeral ceremony? Don't you know that finding God is the funeral of all sorrows? Then why so glum? Don't take this life too seriously." He taught me that one must be mentally above every crucifixion of earthly experience in order to find complete happiness in God.

Krishna taught: "Even-minded during happiness and sorrow, profit and loss, triumph and failure—so encounter the battle of life! Thus thou wilt not acquire sin."* To remain evenminded, no matter what comes, is one of the best ways to conquer delusive desires. This I learned from the example of my great master—even to the last, changeless. Christ also demonstrated that spirit. Even though Jesus was tortured, God's love was not taken away; he did not lose his divine consciousness. God's protection of our joy and peace is the greatest fortress possible. Throughout all trials and sufferings, remember the good things that God has given you. Your soul is a divine temple of God. The darkness of mortal ignorance and limitations must be driven out of that temple. It is wonderful to be in the consciousness of the soul—fortified, strong!

* Bhagavad Gita II:38.

Be afraid of nothing. Hating none, giving love to all, feeling the love of God, seeing His presence in everyone, and having but one desire—for His constant presence in the temple of your consciousness—that is the way to live in this world. Those who have other desires will not know true satisfaction.

Environment Shapes Our Desires

Desires are formed according to one's environment; they are created by, and therefore limited by, your sense perceptions. Attending a country fair satisfies a desire for a little excitement; but after you have been to a world fair and viewed all the different exhibits, a small fair no longer holds any attraction. This illustrates the importance of having communion with God now, for the comparison with inferior earthly joys; then your desires will be of a much higher and more advanced nature. The desire to be one with God is the greatest of all. When you are through with any lesser desire, you soon pick up another, but when you have God, all other desires are satisfied completely. "Seek ye *first* the kingdom of God, and his righteousness; and all these things shall be added unto you."* Why not fulfil first this highest desire? for when He answers your prayer to know Him, all other desires will be instantly fulfilled throughout eternity.

Perhaps you feel that you have no desires. Well, I have often noticed what happens when people go shopping. They may have no particular desire to buy, but suddenly something catches their eye and they think, "I must have it!" Day and night that object is on their mind, and finally they buy it, even if they have to borrow the money. Then, after having it for a while, their happiness in it grows stale,

* *Matthew* 6:33 (Bible).

and they want something else. We meet people who say, "If only I could have a thousand dollars (or a car, or a swimming pool)," and when that wish is satisfied, they yearn for something different. Human desires are not perfect, hence their fulfilment does not lead to perfect happiness.

The world environment will try to prevent you from remembering that the only worthwhile desire is to have God. But every day you should remind yourself of this. And when you have made up your mind not to smoke, or eat unwisely, or lie or cheat, be firm in these good desires; don't weaken. Wrong environment saps your will and invites wrong desires. Live with thieves and you think that is the only life. But live with divine persons, and after having divine communion, no other desires can tempt you. All become stale. Therefore even a few moments of deep meditation, or the company of a saint, will be a raft of inspiration to carry you across this ocean of delusion to the shores of God.

Be Safe in the Castle of God's Presence

Joy lies in continually thinking of God. The longing for Him should be constant. A time comes when your mind never wanders away, when not even the greatest affliction of body, mind, and soul can take your consciousness from the living presence of God. Is that not wonderful? to live and think and feel God all the time? to remain in the castle of His presence, whence death nor aught else can take you away? "On Me fix thy mind, be thou My devotee, with ceaseless worship bow reverently before Me. Having thus united thyself to Me as thy Highest Goal, thou shalt be Mine own."* When you are proof against all desires, you are enjoying the Presence Eternal.

* Bhagavad Gita IX:34.

This life is strange. Everything is subject to change. That is why one should not anchor his happiness on this life. Our time will pass on; what you are seeing now will be gone one day. Change is good if you don't let it hurt you. When it does hurt, the rebellion you feel is meant to show you that you should not have any desires. When you are anchored in that great Spirit you are enjoying everything, but without attachment. Therefore it is worthwhile to make the effort to know Him. Otherwise life can horribly disillusion you.

When I went back to India in 1935, I was looking forward to visiting some of the places I had enjoyed as a child, but upon my arrival I saw everything had changed. The stage was differently set. The greatest disillusionment came to me when I visited my old home in Ichapur, where I used to play and watch the birds. I was shocked. Only one remembered tree was left. That is the way life is; one by one, things familiar and dear vanish from our sight. I would have given anything then to have seen our home as it was in my childhood. Nevertheless I did see it later, materialized in a vision: we swam in the pond, and I went upstairs in the house and lay on the bed and ate mangoes, as I had done so many years before.

Scrutinize your desires carefully now. Sort them and keep only good ones; and let not even those good desires choke off the one important desire, for God. That must not be stifled. You are in great delusion when you ask God for fulfilment of your earthly desires and never ask Him to make a gift of Himself to you. What would you think of a son who says, "Mother, write a check for me," whenever he wants anything, but otherwise gives no thought to her? Don't be like that; never be ungrateful.

When this book of life shall be closed, there will remain with you only the realization gained from those desires you have fulfilled in connection with God. So read from *Whispers** and then meditate before you go to bed each night. When you wake up, think of God. Pray not only before taking food, but when you are eating, and afterward. When you are working, weave the thought of God around that activity. When you are in touch with God, you will see all your desires mysteriously fulfilled. But you must seek Him first. He has given you everything; but only if you forsake all His gifts, preferring Him, will He surrender Himself. When you show God that you are willing to sacrifice everything to know Him, He will come to you.

Carry a Portable Heaven Within

The hardest obstacle to overcome is yourself. When you sit to meditate at night, your nervousness and restlessness are still with you. Learn to control your mind and body. Be king of yourself. Carry within you a portable heaven, and in life or in death, in heaven or in hades, that inner heaven will be with you. Pray deeply, sincerely, "O God, I yearn to know You. You must answer me!" and next morning pray again, "Lord, You must come to me!" and pray again the next night in the same way, in the language of your heart; if you keep on, He must respond. But when you pray halfheartedly, while thinking in the back of your mind about something else, He knows He is not first with you, and He does not respond.

Have God first. Have God now. Don't wait, because delusion is very strong. Before you know it, the time will have come for you to quit this world. Whenever you have

* *Whispers from Eternity,* a book of spiritualized prayers by Paramahansa Yogananda. A spiritualized prayer is one to which God has responded. Any devotee praying deeply and sincerely to Him in those same words will receive a similar blessing. *(Publisher's Note)*

a moment, sit down and meditate. No matter how many times your prayers have not been answered, don't worry; keep on praying. Pray with sincerity. Believe that your prayer is answered.

In my life I have seen the most wonderful demonstrations of God's response to prayer. I urge you to pray not for little things, but for His presence. Only that prayer is worthwhile. If you are willing to sacrifice an hour or two of sleep for meditation every night, you will enter the kingdom of God. Don't watch the time. With deep sincerity pray, "Lord, I want You alone." Bad habits and restlessness will try to shake you from your effort, but keep your mind on God and you will find His presence with you.

Desires for worldly joys create the magnetic attraction that draws man back to earth, life after life. Reincarnation is no longer necessary for those who have fulfilled their desires in God. Whenever they want to fulfil any wish, they simply think of that object and it is materialised before them. My mother appeared before me in flesh and blood, just as I see you here. How kind is God, how marvellous is God! that He materializes the objects of our desires to show us His love and gratefulness when we have given Him first place in our hearts.

To be able to demonstrate health or wealth or power or friends with God's help is fine, but if you can coax God Himself to respond to your prayers, you are a man of destiny. So don't rest until you demonstrate God in your life. He will give you everything you ever wished for; and He will test you. The tests in the spiritual life are greater than in any other. But you who pass His tests shall say: "Lord, my greatest prayer has been answered. What else could my heart want or need, but You?"

Paramahansa Yogananda: A Yogi in Life and Death

Paramahansa Yogananda entered *mahasamadhi* (a yogi's final conscious exit from the body) in Los Angeles, California, on March 7, 1952, after concluding his speech at a banquet held in honour of H. E. Binay R. Sen, Ambassador of India.

The great world teacher demonstrated the value of yoga (scientific techniques for God-realization) not only in life but in death. Weeks after his departure his unchanged face shone with the divine lustre of incorruptibility.

Mr. Harry T. Rowe, Los Angeles Mortuary Director, Forest Lawn Memorial-Park (in which the body of the great master is temporarily placed), sent Self-Realization Fellowship a notarized letter from which the following extracts are taken:

"The absence of any visual signs of decay in the dead body of Paramahansa Yogananda offers the most extraordinary case in our experience....No physical disintegration was visible in his body even twenty days after death....No indication of mould was visible on his skin, and no visible desiccation (drying up) took place in the bodily tissues. This state of perfect preservation of a body is, so far as we know from mortuary annals, an unparalleled one....At the time of receiving Yogananda's body, the Mortuary personnel expected to observe, through the glass lid of the casket, the usual progressive signs of bodily decay. Our astonishment increased as day followed day without bringing any visible change in the body under observation. Yogananda's body was apparently in a phenomenal state of immutability....

"No odour of decay emanated from his body at any time....The physical appearance of Yogananda on March 27th, just before the bronze cover of the casket was put into position, was the same as it had been on March 7th. He looked on March 27th as fresh and as unravaged by decay as he had looked on the night of his death. On March 27th there was no reason to say that his body had suffered any visible physical disintegration at all. For these reasons we state again that the case of Paramahansa Yogananda is unique in our experience."

Aims And Ideals

of

Yogoda Satsanga Society of India

As set forth by

Sri Sri Paramahansa Yogananda, Gurudeva and Founder

Sri Sri Swami Chidananda Giri, President

To disseminate among the nations a knowledge of definite scientific techniques for attaining direct personal experience of God.

To teach that the purpose of life is the evolution, through self-effort, of man's limited mortal consciousness into God Consciousness; and to this end to establish Yogoda Satsanga temples for God-communion, and to encourage the establishment of individual temples of God in the homes and in the hearts of men.

To reveal the complete harmony and basic oneness of original Yoga as taught by Bhagavan Krishna and original Christianity as taught by Jesus Christ; and to show that these principles of truth are the common scientific foundation of all true religions.

To point out the one divine highway to which all paths of true religious beliefs eventually lead: the highway of daily, scientific, devotional meditation on God.

To liberate man from his threefold suffering: physical disease, mental inharmonies, and spiritual ignorance.

To encourage "plain living and high thinking"; and to spread a spirit of brotherhood among all peoples by teaching the eternal basis of their unity: kinship with God.

To demonstrate the superiority of mind over body, of soul over mind.

To overcome evil by good, sorrow by joy, cruelty by kindness, ignorance by wisdom.

To unite science and religion through realization of the unity of their underlying principles.

To advocate cultural and spiritual understanding between East and West, and the exchange of their finest distinctive features.

To serve mankind as one's larger Self.

Books by Paramahansa Yogananda

- Autobiography of a Yogi
- The Divine Romance
- Inner Peace
- Where There Is Light
- The Law of Success
- Living Fearlessly
- Songs of the Soul
- The Science of Religion
- To be Victorious in Life
- Nervousness: Cause and Cure
- Seek God Now
- The Universality of Yoga
- Man's Eternal Quest
- Journey to Self-realization
- In the Sanctuary of the Soul
- Whispers from Eternity
- How you can talk with God
- Metaphysical Meditations
- Wine of the Mystic
- Words of Cosmic Chants
- Developing Dynamic Will
- The Art of Living
- Who Made God?
- Man's Greatest Adventure
- Scientific Healing Affirmations
- Increasing the Power of Initiative
- Sayings of Paramahansa Yogananda
- Why God Permits Evil and How to Rise Above It
- Autobiography of a Yogi (MP3 Audiobook, read *by Sir Ben Kingsley*)
- God Talks with Arjuna: The Bhagavad Gita (A New Translation and Commentary)
- The Second Coming of Christ: The Resurrection of the Christ Within You—A Revelatory Commentary on the Original Teachings of Jesus

Other Publications From Yogoda Satsanga Society of India

- The Holy Science *by Sri Sri Swami Sri Yukteswar Giri*
- Paramahansa Yogananda: In Memoriam—Personal Accounts of the Master's Final Days
- Rajarsi Janakananda—A Great Western Yogi
- Only Love: Living the Spiritual Life in a Changing World *by Sri Sri Daya Mata*
- Finding the Joy Within You: Personal Counsel for God-Centred Living *by Sri Sri Daya Mata*
- Enter the Quiet Heart: Creating a Loving Relationship With God *by Sri Sri Daya Mata*
- Intuition: Soul-Guidance for Life's Decisions *by Sri Sri Daya Mata*

- Manifesting Divine Consciousness in Daily Life *by Sri Sri Mrinalini Mata*
- Visiting the Saints of India With Sri Daya Mata *by Sri Mrinalini Mata*
- God Alone: The Life and Letters of a Saint *by Sri Gyanamata*
- "Mejda": The Family and the Early Life of Sri Sri Paramahansa Yogananda *by Sananda Lal Ghosh*
- Spiritual Diary
- Two Frogs in Trouble
- Yogoda Satsanga Magazine
- Paramahansa Yogananda—A Saint for East and West (An Amar Chitra Katha Publication)

Audio Recordings of Paramahansa Yogananda

- Awake in the Cosmic Dream
- Beholding the One in All
- The Great Light of God
- Be a Smile Millionaire
- In the Glory of Spirit
- To Make Heaven on Earth
- One Life Versus Reincarnation
- Removing All Sorrow and Suffering
- Self-Realization: The Inner and the Outer Path
- Songs of My Heart (Chants, Poems, and Prayers)

Informal Talks by Other Disciples of Paramahansa Yogananda

Sri Sri Daya Mata

- A Heart Aflame
- Finding God in Daily Life
- God First
- Anchoring Your Life in God
- Free Yourself from Tension
- Let Us Be Thankful
- Living a God Centred Life
- Moral Courage: Effecting Positive Change Through Moral and Spiritual Choices
- "My Spirit Shall Live On..." The Final Days of Sri Sri Paramahansa Yogananda
- Strengthening the Power of the Mind
- A Blessing From Mahavatar Babaji
- Attuning Our Lives to the Guru's Blessings
- Is Meditation on God Compatible with Modern Life?
- Karma Yoga: Balancing Activity and Meditation
- The Way to Peace, Humility, and Love for God
- Understanding the Soul's Need for God

Sri Sri Mrinalini Mata

- ❖ If You Would Know the Guru: Remembrances of Life With Sri Sri Paramahansa Yogananda
- ❖ Living in Attunement with the Divine
- ❖ Look Always to the Light
- ❖ The Guru: Messenger of Truth
- ❖ The Interior Life
- ❖ Embracing and Sharing the Universal Love of God
- ❖ The Yoga Sadhana That Brings God's Love and Bliss

Swami Anandamoy Giri

- ❖ Is Peace Possible in Today's World?
- ❖ Kriya Yoga: Portal to the Infinite
- ❖ Loyalty: The Highest Spiritual Law
- ❖ The Importance of a True Guru
- ❖ Devotion: Understanding Its Deeper Aspects in the Search for God
- ❖ Kriya Yoga: Divine Dispensation for Our Awakening Age

Swami Smarananda Giri

- ❖ Banat, Banat, Ban Jai
- ❖ Deepening Our Practice of Meditation

Swami Mokshananda Giri

- ❖ Remembrances of the Guru, Sri Sri Paramahansa Yogananda

DVDs

- ❖ The Life of Sri Sri Paramahansa Yogananda: The Early Years in America (1920-1928)
- ❖ Finding Divine Peace and Balance *by Sri Sri Daya Mata*
- ❖ Him I Shall Follow *by Sri Sri Daya Mata*
- ❖ Living in the Love of God *by Sri Sri Daya Mata*
- ❖ Opening Your Heart to God's Presence *by Sri Sri Daya Mata*
- ❖ Security in a World of Change *by Sri Sri Daya Mata*
- ❖ The Love and Wisdom of Sri Sri Paramahansa Yogananda *by Sri Sri Daya Mata*
- ❖ Be Messengers of God's Light and Love *by Sri Sri Mrinalini Mata*
- ❖ In His Presence: Remembrances of Life With Sri Sri Paramahansa Yogananda *by Sri Sri Mrinalini Mata*

- Portal to the Inner Light: Official Release of Paramahansa Yogananda's The Second Coming of Christ: The Resurrection of the Christ Within You *by Sri Sri Mrinalini Mata*
- Experiencing God Within *by Swami Anandamoy Giri*
- The Wisdom of the Bhagavad Gita *by Swami Anandamoy Giri*
- You Can Know God in This Life *by Swami Anandamoy Giri*
- Your Thoughts Can Change Your Life *by Swami Anandamoy Giri*

Bhajans sung by Brahmacharini Mirabai:

- Anjali
- Jai Ma (Set of 2 CDs)
- Shanti Mandir (Set of 2 CDs)
- Arpan (Set of 2 CDs)

Devotional Chants sung by Sannyasis of YSS:

- Atma Ki Pukar

Some of the above-mentioned books are also published in Assamese, Bengali, Gujarati, Hindi, Kannada, Malayalam, Marathi, Nepali, Odia, Punjabi, Sanskrit, Sinhala, Tamil, Telugu, and Urdu. For a complete list of books and audio / video recordings visit our online store at the address given below. Also available are black-and-white and colour pictures of Sri Sri Paramahansa Yogananda.

Available at your local bookstore or from:

Yogoda Satsanga Society of India
Paramahansa Yogananda Path
Ranchi 834001, Jharkhand
Tel.: (0651) 6655 555
bookstore.yssofindia.org

Yogoda Satsanga Lessons in Self-realization

Personal guidance and instructions from Paramahansa Yogananda on the techniques of yoga meditation and principles of spiritual living

If you feel drawn to the spiritual truths described in *Habit—Your Master or Your Slave?*, we invite you to enrol in the *Yogoda Satsanga Lessons.*

Paramahansa Yogananda originated this home-study series to provide sincere seekers the opportunity to learn and practise the ancient yoga meditation techniques introduced in this book—including the science of *Kriya Yoga*. The *Lessons* also present his practical guidance for attaining balanced physical, mental and spiritual well-being.

The *Yogoda Satsanga Lessons* are available at a nominal fee (to cover printing and postage costs). All students are freely given personal guidance in their practice by Yogoda Satsanga Society of India monks.

For more information...

Please visit www.ysslessons.org to request a comprehensive complimentary information packet about the *Lessons,* which includes:

- *"An Overview of the Yogoda Satsanga Lessons in Self-realization: Information About Paramahansa Yogananda's Home-Study Series"*
- *"Highest Achievements Through Self-realization," by Paramahansa Yogananda—a thorough introduction to the teachings presented in the YSS Lessons*

By the same author...

Autobiography of a Yogi

by Sri Sri Paramahansa Yogananda

This acclaimed autobiography is at once a riveting account of an extraordinary life and a penetrating and unforgettable look at the ultimate mysteries of human existence. Hailed as a landmark work of spiritual literature when it first appeared in print, it remains one of the most widely read and respected books ever published on the wisdom of the East.

With engaging candour, eloquence, and wit, Sri Sri Paramahansa Yogananda narrates the inspiring chronicle of his life—the experiences of his remarkable childhood, encounters with many saints and sages during his youthful search throughout India for an illumined teacher, ten years of training in the hermitage of a revered yoga master, and the thirty years that he lived and taught in America. He records as well his meetings with Mahatma Gandhi, Rabindranath Tagore, Luther Burbank, the Catholic stigmatist Therese Neumann, and other celebrated spiritual personalities of East and West. Also included is extensive material that he added after the first edition came out in 1946, with a final chapter on the closing years of his life.

Considered a modern spiritual classic, *Autobiography of a Yogi* offers a profound introduction to the ancient science of Yoga. It has been translated into more than fifty languages and is widely used in college and university courses. A perennial best-seller since it was first published over seventy years ago, *Autobiography of a Yogi* has found its way into the hearts of millions of readers around the world.

"The Autobiography of this sage makes captivating reading." —The Times of India

"A rare account." —The New York Times

"A fascinating and clearly annotated study." —Newsweek

"There has been nothing before, written in English or in any other European language, like this presentation of Yoga." —Columbia University Press